NORMAN DELLO JOIO

PIANO MUSIC

AMP 8203
First Printing: June 2007

ISBN-13: 978-0-634-09627-3
ISBN-10: 0-634-09627-3

Associated Music Publishers, Inc.

DISTRIBUTED BY

CORPORATION
7777 W. BLUEMOUND RD. P.O. BOX 13819 MILWAUKEE, WI 53213

www.schirmer.com
www.halleonard.com

NORMAN DELLO JOIO

The distinguished musical career of Norman Dello Joio began at age 14 when he became a church organist and choir director of the Star of the Sea Church on City Island, New York. A descendant of Italian church organists, he was born on January 24, 1913 in New York. His father was an organist, pianist, singer, and vocal coach. Dello Joio recalls that his father was working with singers from the Metropolitan Opera who used to arrive in their Rolls Royces, and that his childhood was surrounded with musicians and music in the home. Dello Joio's father taught him the piano at age four, and in his teens he began studying organ with his godfather, Pietro Yon, organist at St. Patrick's Cathedral and composer of the Christmas standard "Gesù Bambino." In 1939, he was accepted as a scholarship student at the Juilliard School, and studied composition with Bernard Wagenaar.

As a graduate student at Juilliard, while he was organist at St. Anne's Church in New York, he reached the conclusion that he did not want to spend his life in a church choir loft, as compostion began to envelop all of his interest. In 1941, he began studies with Paul Hindemith, who profoundly influenced his compositional style, at Tanglewood and Yale. It was Hindemith who told Dello Joio, "Your music is lyrical by nature, don't ever forget that." Dello Joio stated that, although he did not completely understand at the time, he later knew what he meant: "Don't sacrifice necessarily to a system, go to yourself, what you hear. If it's valid, and it's good, put it down in your mind. Don't say I have to do this because the system tells me to. No, that's a mistake."

In the latter part of the 1940s, Dello Joio was considered one of America's leading composers and by the 1950s had gained international recognition. He received numerous awards and grants including the Elizabeth Sprague Coolidge Award, the Town Hall Composition Award, two Guggenheim Fellowships, and a grant from the American Academy of Arts and Letters. He won the New York Music Critics' Circle Award in 1948, and again in 1962. He won the Pulitzer Prize in 1957 for *Meditations on Ecclesiastes* for string orchestra, and an Emmy Award for his music in the television special *Scenes from the Louvre*. In 1958, CBS featured him in a one-hour television special, "Profile of a Composer."

A prolific composer, Dello Joio's compositions include over 45 choral works, close to 30 works for orchestra and 10 for band, approximately 25 pieces for solo voice, 20 chamber works, concertos for piano, flute, harp, the *Concertante for Clarinet*, and the *Concertino for Harmonica*. His stage works include three operas (one written for television and revised for the stage) and eight ballets. Additionally, he has written nine television scores and three compositions for organ. His published solo piano works include three sonatas, two nocturnes, two preludes, two suites, two *Songs without Words*, the *Capriccio, Introduction and Fantasies on a Chorale Tune, Diversions, Short Intervallic Etudes*, and Concert Variants. Dello Joio has one published work for piano and orchestra, the *Fantasy and Variations for Piano and Orchestra*. He has also written a number of pedagogical pieces for both two and four hands.

Dello Joio taught at Sarah Lawrence College, the Mannes College of Music, and was Professor of Music and Dean of the Fine and Applied Arts School of Boston University. From 1959 until 1973, he directed the Ford Foundation's Contemporary Music Project, which placed young composers in high schools who were salaried to compose music for school ensembles and programs. The project placed about 90 composers, many of whom successfully continued their careers. In 2007, at the age of 94, Dello Joio continues to compose with no signs of retiring. He is frequently commissioned, and his music remains in constant demand.

CONTENTS

NORMAN DELLO JOIO

PIANO MUSIC

CONCERT VARIANTS FOR PIANO

Theme

Norman Dello Joio

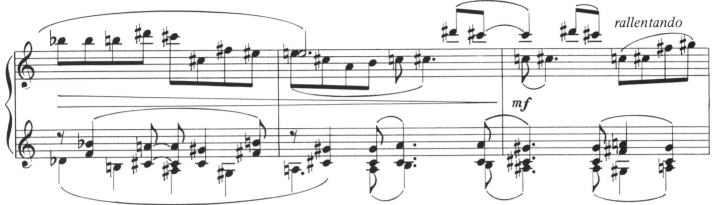

Variant I

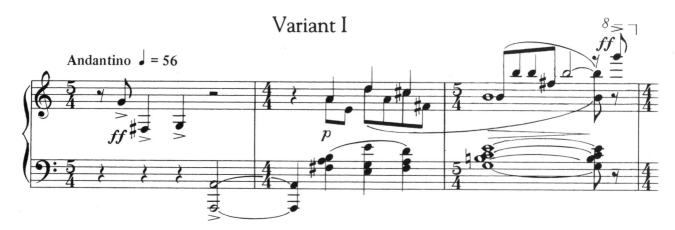

Variant II

Allegro, molto animato ♩. = 104

p *sempre spumante*

non legato

f

p

marcato

ff *feroce*

rallentando poco a poco

(Meno mosso ♩. = 84)

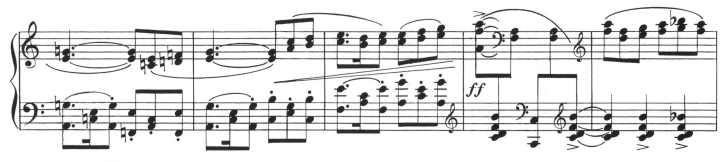

Variant IV

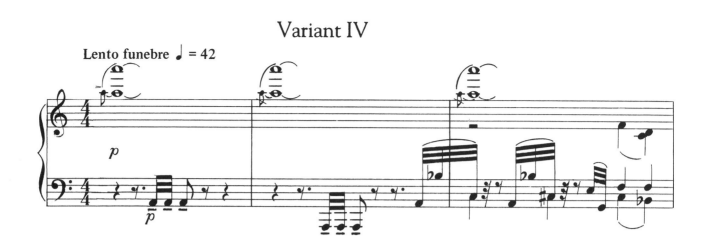

Variant V

Allegro, molto animato ♩. = 72

ARIETTA
from
DIVERSIONS

Norman Dello Joio

semplice cantabile

Andante commodo (♩ = 63)

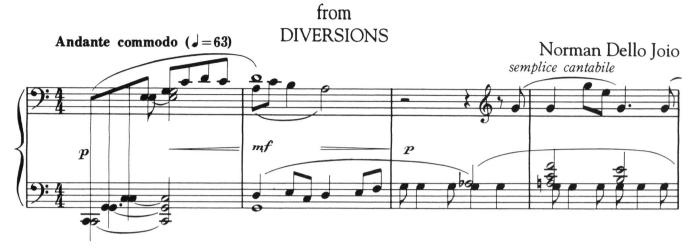

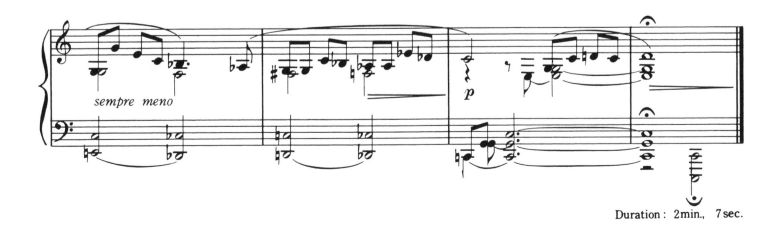

Duration : 2 min., 7 sec.

GIGA
from
DIVERSIONS

Norman Dello Joio

Allegro gioioso (♩.=120)

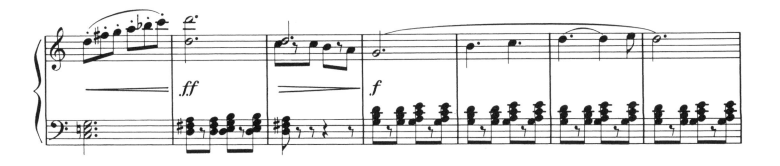

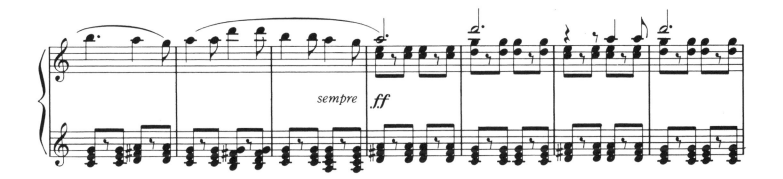

Duration : 1min., 45sec.

CACCIA
from
DIVERSIONS

Norman Dello Joio

Allegro animato (♩ = 92)

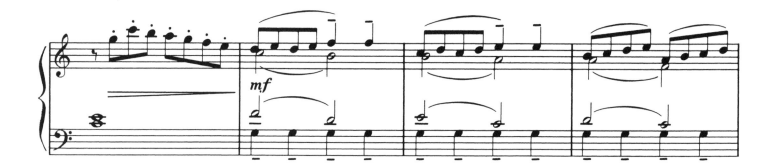

34

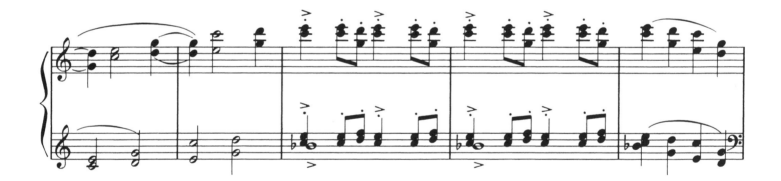

Duration · 1 min., 45 sec.

PRELUDE: TO A YOUNG DANCER

Norman Dello Joio

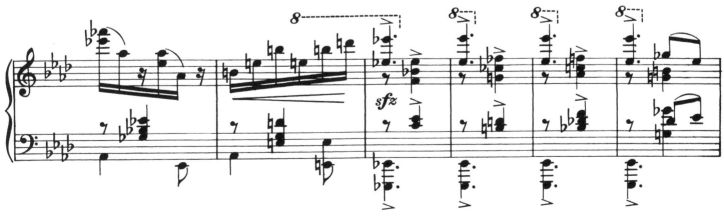

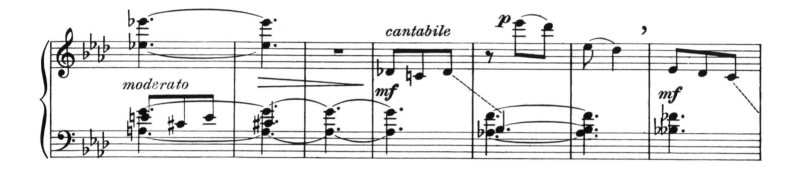

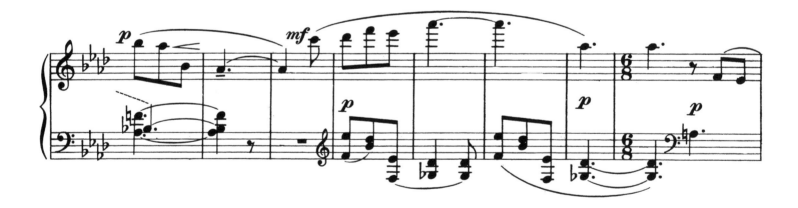

Oct. 19-21, 1945, Wilton, Conn.

PRELUDE: TO A YOUNG MUSICIAN

Norman Dello Joio

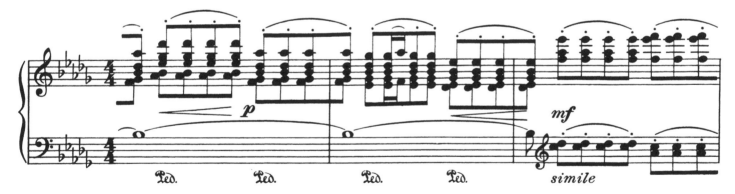

42

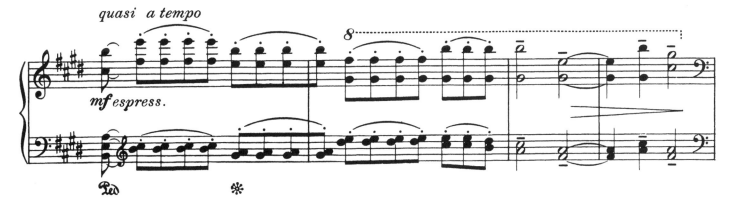

June 15-16, '44

INTRODUCTION AND FANTASIES
ON A CHORALE TUNE

Introduction and Chorale

Norman Dello Joio

Fantasy I

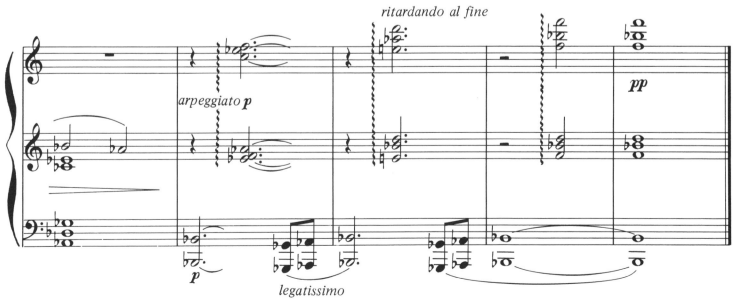

Fantasy II

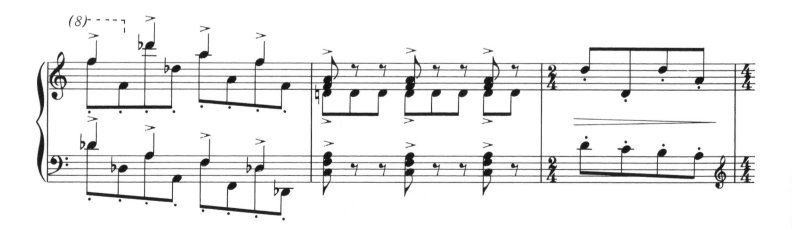

un poco rallentando *a tempo*

cantando la melodia

mf *p leggiero*

f

ff *Vuota* *sempre cantando* *mf con calore*

f *ff con passione*

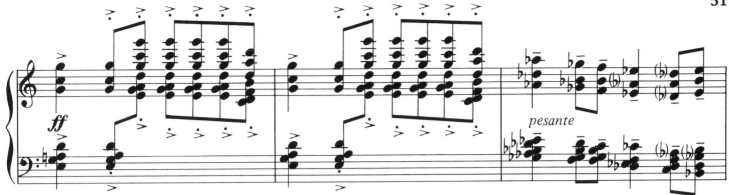

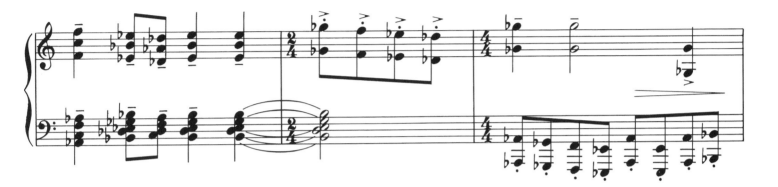

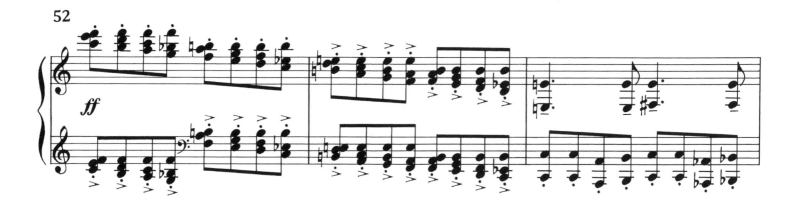

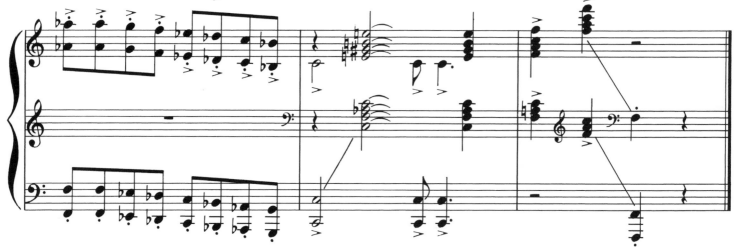

Fantasy III

rallentando

a tempo

p   *ff*   *pesante*

mf   *p*

ritardando e diminuendo al fine

pp

Fantasy IV

Allegro assai, scherzevole ♩=126

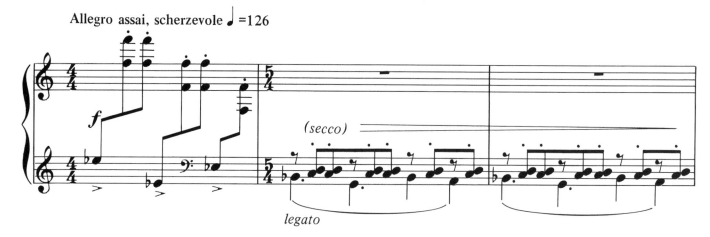

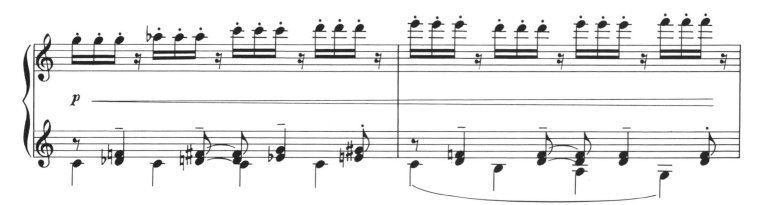

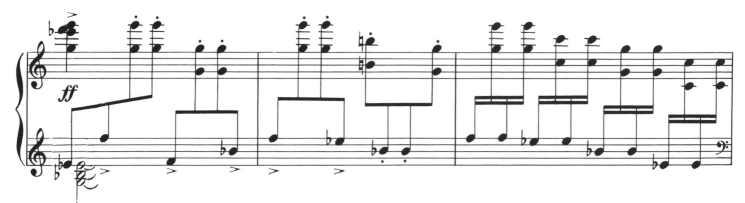

sempre con energia

feroce

crescendo con tutta forza

ben cantando e legato la melodia del Chorale

pesante

sempre cantabile la melodia

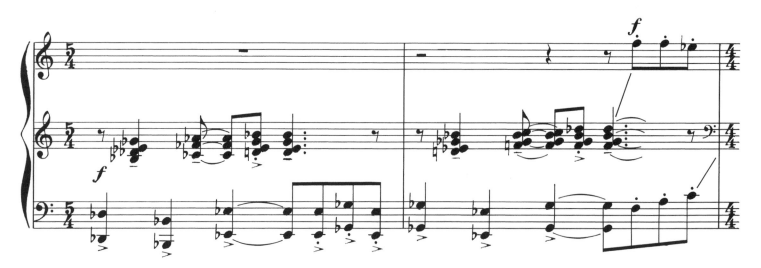

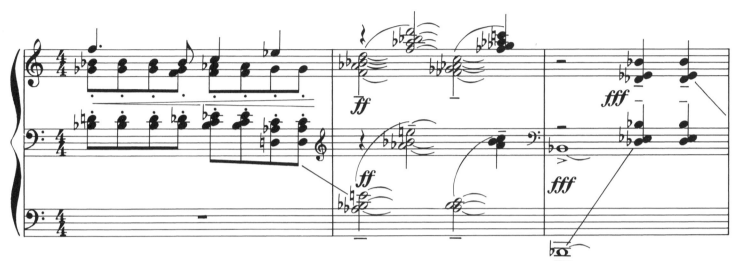

PRAYER OF THE MATADOR

from

LYRIC PIECES FOR THE YOUNG

Norman Dello Joio

Very slow, ♩ = 46-48

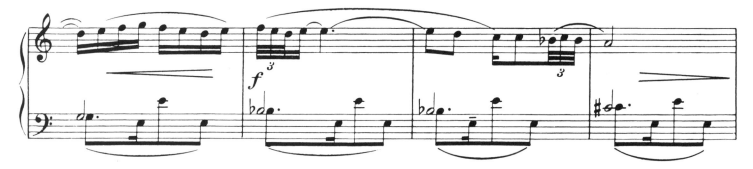

63

Duration: 2 min.

NIGHT SONG

from
LYRIC PIECES FOR THE YOUNG

Norman Dello Joio

Slow and very sustained, ♩ = 56

legato the bass line

cantabile

cantabile

r.h.

legato sempre

sostenuto

legato sempre

Duration: **3** min., **40** sec.

RUSSIAN DANCER
from
LYRIC PIECES FOR THE YOUNG

Norman Dello Joio

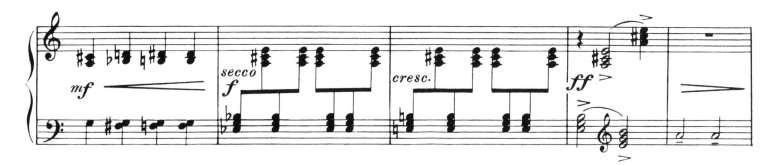

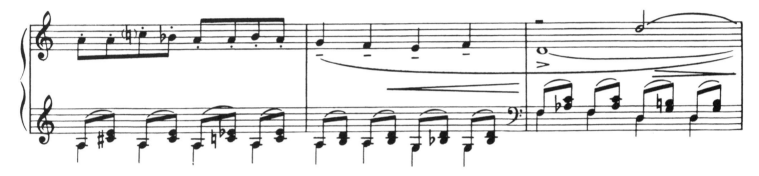

Duration: 2 min. 10 sec.

SALUTE TO SCARLATTI
A Suite of Sonatas
for Piano or Harpsichord

Norman Dello Joio

I

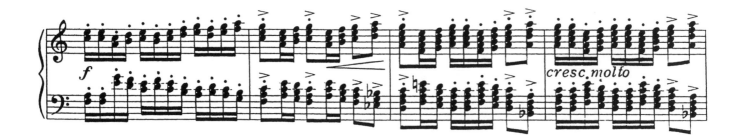

II

III

Allegro moderato e grazioso ♩ = 76

poco rallentando　　*poco meno tempo*

cantabile

accelerando al primo tempo　　Tempo primo

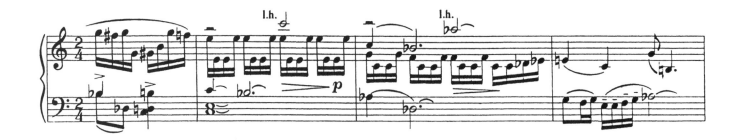

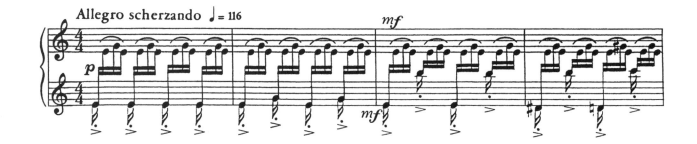

IV

accelerando a tempo primo

SUITE FOR PIANO

Norman Dello Joio

I

II

Bright ♩ = 132

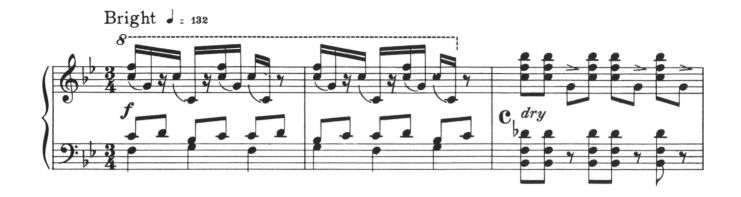

III

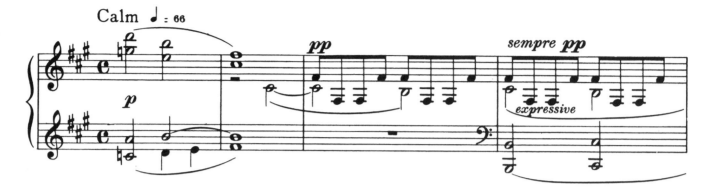

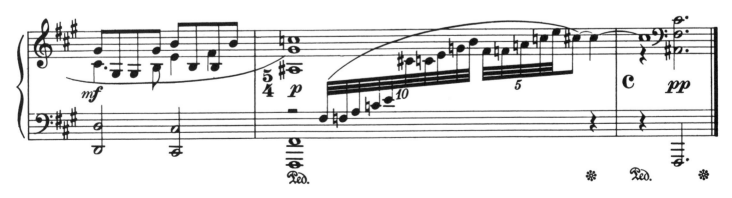

IV

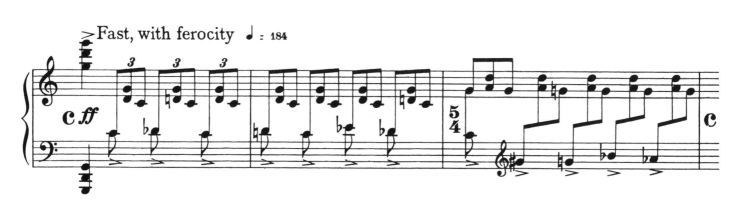

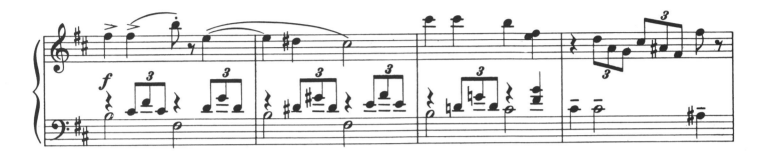

88

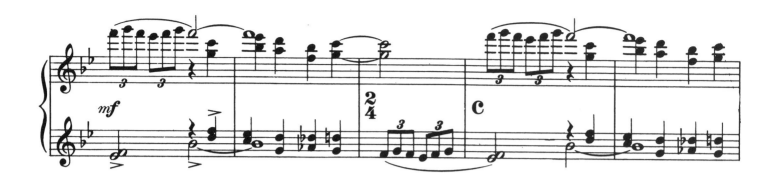

Spring 1940

SHORT INTERVALLIC ETUDES
for Well Tempered Pianists

1/4's and 1/5's

Andante cantabile ♪=84

Norman Dello Joio

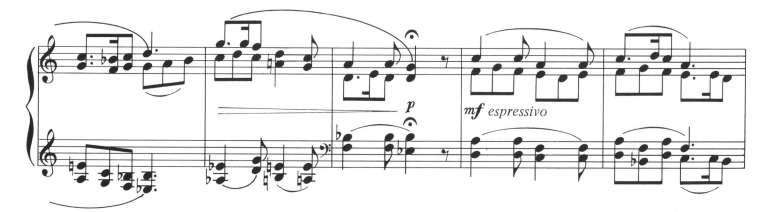

1/3's

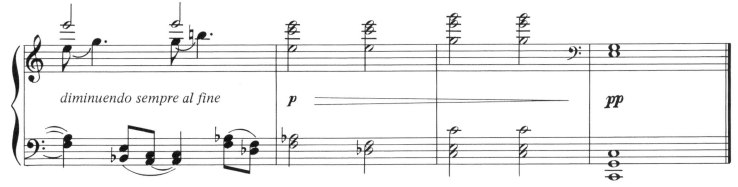

2nds

Allegro scherzando ♩=116

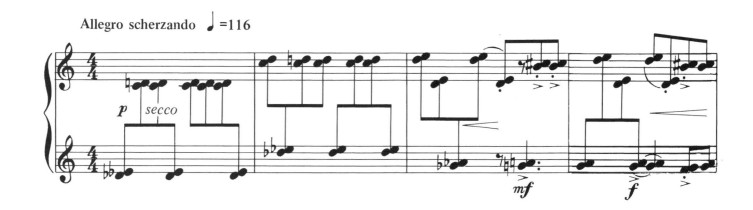

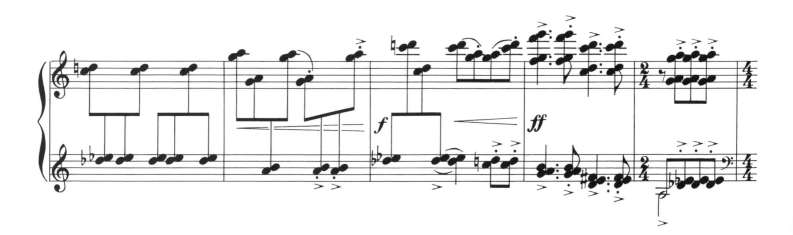

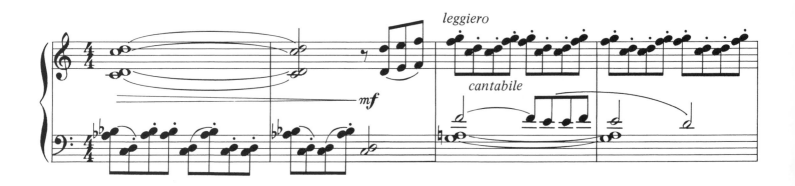

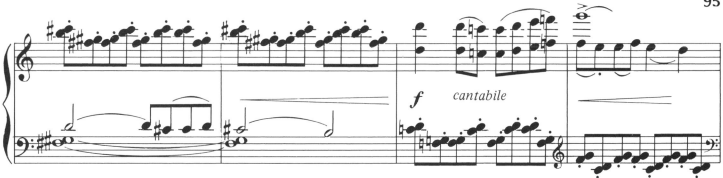

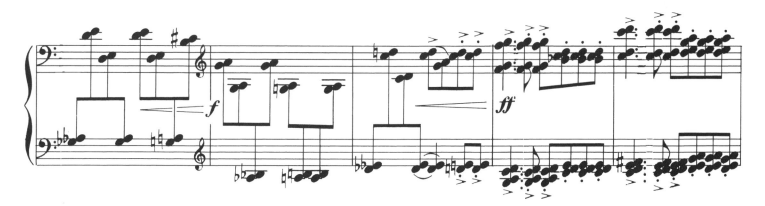

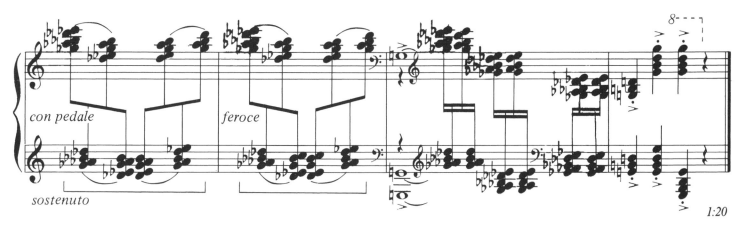

1:20

1/6's

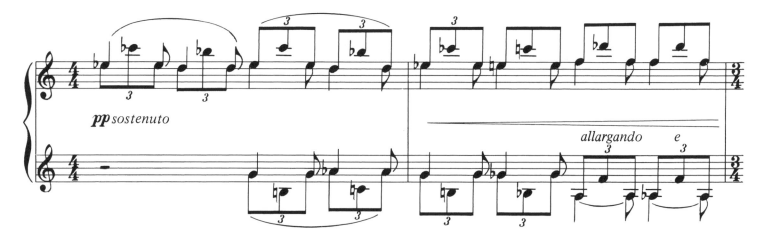

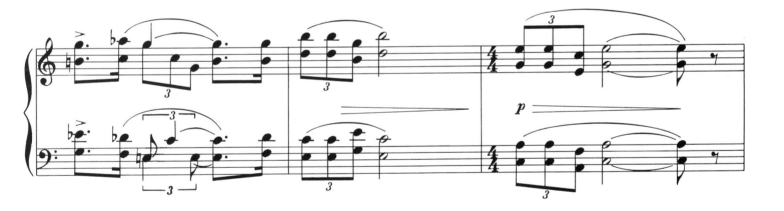

1/7's

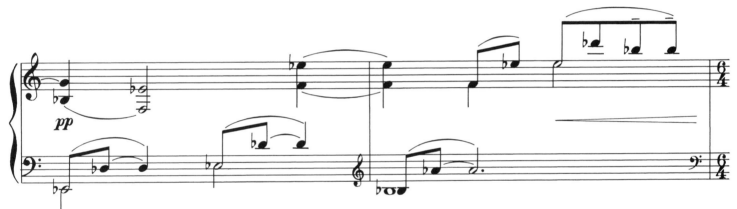

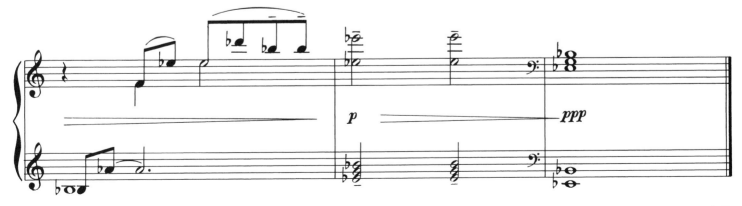

8ves and Unisons

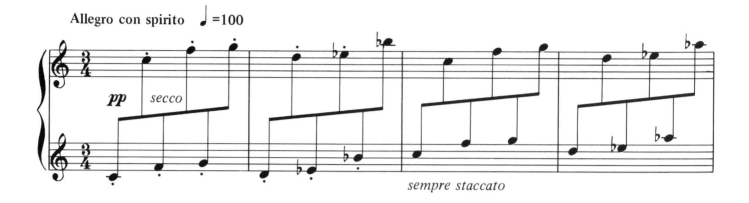

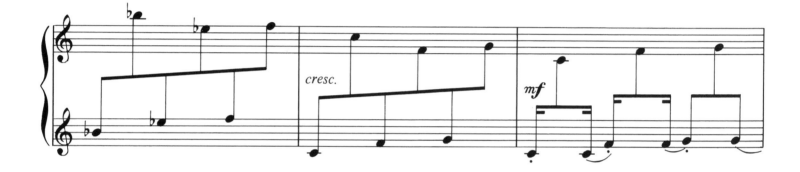

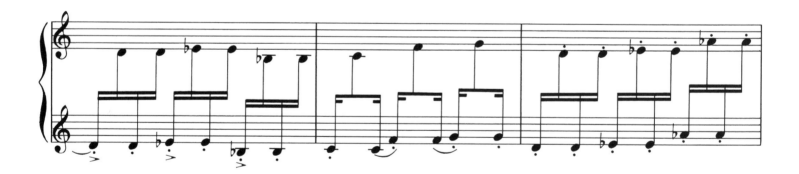

subito *p* e spumante — sempre leggiero

martellato — sempre con energia

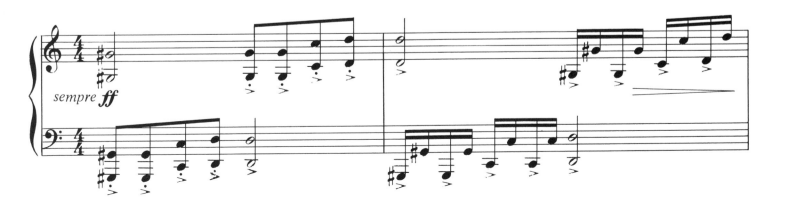

sempre **ff**

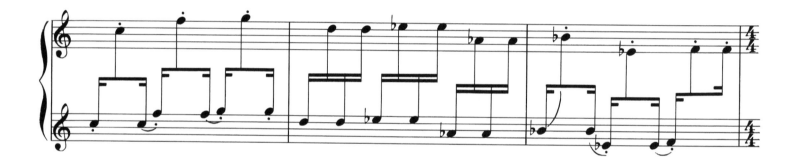

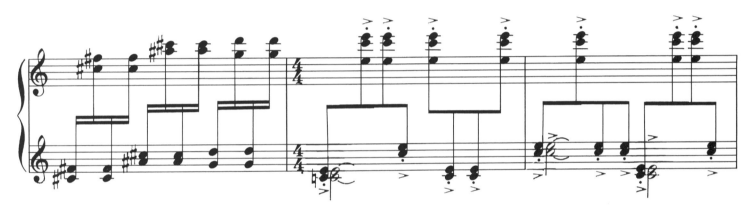

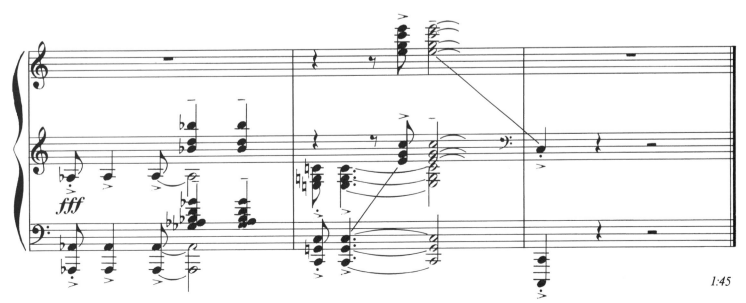

to my Barbara

ALLEGRETTO

from
SIMPLE SKETCHES

Norman Dello Joio

allargando molto _ _ _ _ _ _ _ _ _ **a tempo** ♩ = 90

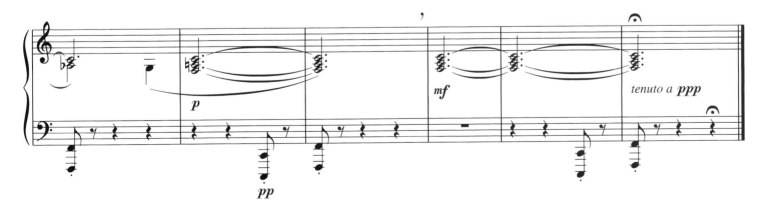

SONATA NO. 2

I

Norman Dello Joio

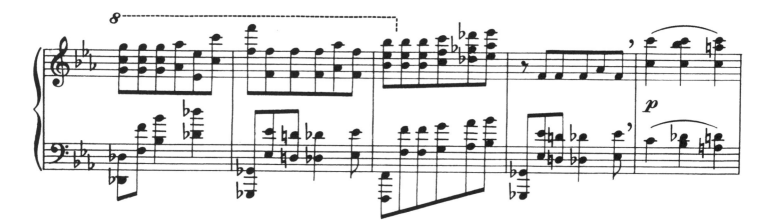

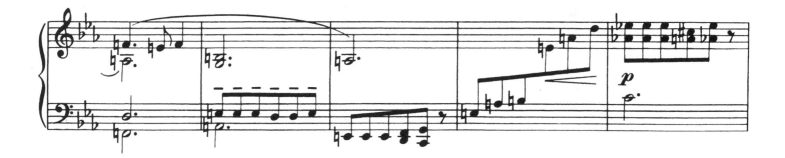

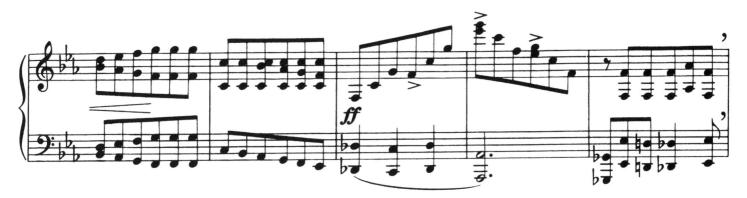

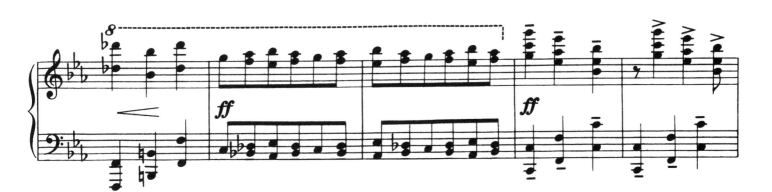

II

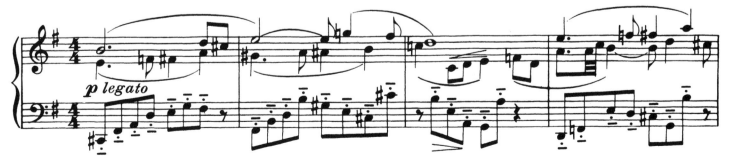

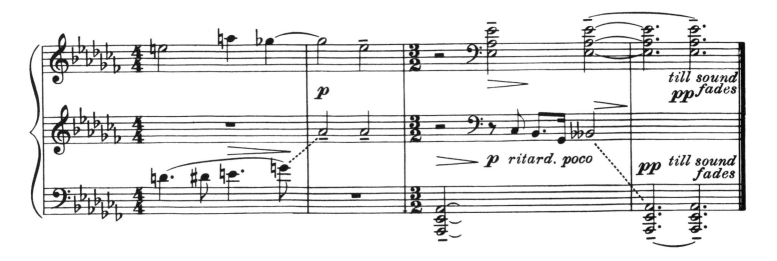

III

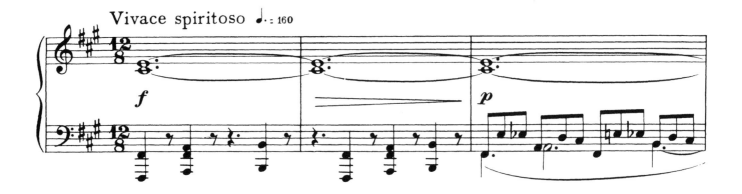

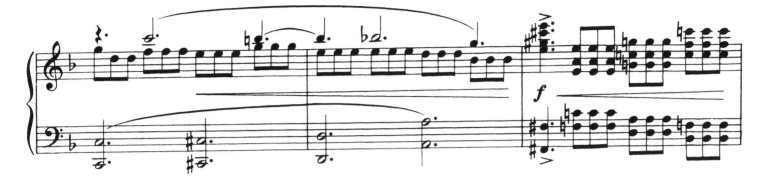

Doppio movimento

Sept. 2-29, 1948